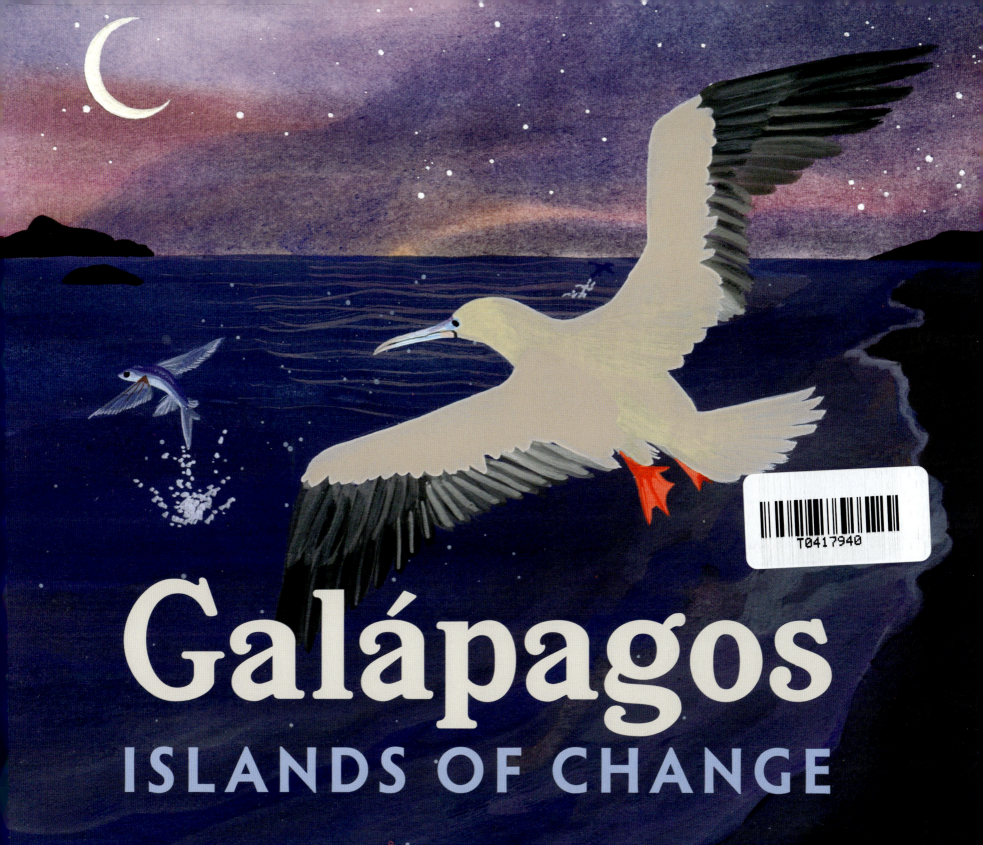

Galápagos
ISLANDS OF CHANGE

For Willa, Rosalind, and Zelda
—L. B.

Published by
PEACHTREE PUBLISHING COMPANY INC.
1700 Chattahoochee Avenue
Atlanta, Georgia 30318-2112
PeachtreeBooks.com

Text © 2023 by Leslie Bulion
Illustrations © 2023 by Becca Stadtlander

First trade paperback edition published in 2025

Edited by Vicky Holifield
Design and composition by Adela Pons

The illustrations were created in gouache and pastels.

Printed and bound in December 2024 at R.R. Donnelley, DongGuan, China.
10 9 8 7 6 5 4 3 2 1 (hardcover)
10 9 8 7 6 5 4 3 2 1 (trade paperback)
HC ISBN: 978-1-68263-496-7
PB ISBN: 978-1-68263-785-2

Library of Congress Cataloging-in-Publication Data

Names: Bulion, Leslie, 1958- author. | Stadtlander, Becca, illustrator.
Title: Galápagos : islands of change / written by Leslie Bulion ; illustrated by Becca Stadtlander.
Description: First edition. | Atlanta, Georgia : Peachtree Publishing Company Inc., [2023] | Includes bibliographical references and index. | Audience: Ages 8-12 | Audience: Grades 4-6 | Summary: "A poetic introduction to a distinctive island ecosystem that is home to many species found nowhere else on Earth" — Provided by publisher.
Identifiers: LCCN 2022044130 | ISBN 9781682634967 (hardcover) | ISBN 9781682635209 (ebook)
Subjects: LCSH: Island ecology—Galapagos Islands—Juvenile literature. | Animal ecology—Galapagos Islands—Juvenile literature.
Classification: LCC QH541.5.I8 B85 2023 | DDC 577.5/2098665—dc23/eng/20221207
LC record available at https://lccn.loc.gov/2022044130

EU Authorized Representative: HackettFlynn Ltd, 36 Cloch Choirneal, Balrothery, Co. Dublin, K32 C942, Ireland. EU@walkerpublishinggroup.com

Galápagos

ISLANDS OF CHANGE

Written by **LESLIE BULION** | Illustrated by **BECCA STADTLANDER**

PEACHTREE

ATLANTA

Galápagos:
Islands at the Crossroads

In a fiery flash, a volcanic hotspot erupts through the sea floor near the equator in the eastern Pacific Ocean. Molten lava settles and cools. With each burst, the volcano builds upward until its cone rises above the waves: a new island is born. Time passes, Earth's rocky outer layer shifts, and the same deep hotspot spews lava — sometimes accompanied by rocks and ash — to build a new volcano, then another. These volcanoes form a cluster of islands: the archipelago known as the Galápagos Islands.

Some of the first plants and animals to reach the bare lava shores ride winds for hundreds of miles to cross the Pacific from South America. Lightweight seeds, insects, and seabirds built for long-distance flight are the only accidental air travelers to succeed. Swift ocean currents sweep marine mammals and other strong swimmers toward the islands. Reptiles with tough hides raft across the salty Pacific on mats of floating debris. Only a small, odd assortment of organisms survives the difficult journey.

Over millions of years these castaways adapt to each island's changing volcanic landscape, seasonal weather, and new community of organisms. Isolated from the mainland and from some of the other islands, many Galápagos animals and plants evolve into endemic species — unique forms of life found nowhere else on Earth.

Nearly every year between July and December, steady winds send cold, deep currents rushing across the Pacific Ocean toward the Galápagos. The undersea currents hit the islands and follow volcanic slopes upward into surface waters. Tiny phytoplankton near the ocean's surface and seaweeds use nutrients carried in cold, deep currents to turn sunlight into food energy. These primary producers support the entire ocean food web, from the smallest animal swimmers called zooplankton to predatory Galápagos sharks. Many shore dwellers such as marine iguanas, penguins, and sea lions also rely on food energy from the ocean.

Near the first of the year, winds shift, cold currents weaken, and warmer waters surround the islands. Warmed air over the ocean rises, bringing the regular rains of the Galápagos wet season. Land plants flourish, including the prickly pear cactus upon which many island birds, reptiles, and insects depend. With few land mammals able to survive those long-ago crossings, a giant centipede has become a surprising and mighty predator. The Galápagos hawk enjoys prey of all sizes from its perch atop the land food web.

Straddling the equator, at the crossroads of ocean currents and volcanoes, the Galápagos ecosystem faces increasing challenges from one of the archipelago's most recent arrivals: humans.

Cool Ocean . . .

When steady trade winds sweep the vast Pacific,
cool currents *whoosh* below,
crossing thousands of miles,
until *crash!*
they meet deep slopes
of volcanic isles
and rush uphill—

u p w e l l i n g

These poems celebrate remarkable animals and plants across the entire Galápagos ecosystem. Each island has its own community of species.

spilling chilled, nourishing waters
through sun-sparkle seas,
helping tiny floating phytoplankton
use sunlight to flourish,
and fresh seaweeds to spread and grow
over tumbles of lava boulders
fringing Galápagos shores and shallows.

Cold, deep-ocean waters carry important nutrients that phytoplankton and seaweeds need to produce food energy, using energy from the sun during photosynthesis.

. . . Dry Season

Overcast skies.
Ocean-cooled air hovers,
trapped by warm air above it,
unable to rise.

Day by day,
dry by dry,
island plants must bid goodbye
to cloudburst downpours.

Across volcanic slopes,
across lowlands and coast,
lush leafy greens
hush to grays, browns, and creams.

La garúa—the cool sea mist—
sifts across the islands' highlands,
catching tip-top branches of giant daisy trees,
then
       drip,
          drip,
             dropping
onto thirsty ferns and mosses
in the moist forest understory.

Giant daisy trees form a moist cloud
forest zone on taller islands.

Phytoplankton

Transparent geometric forms
trap sun to help the oceans bloom
with food for zooplankton swarms.

The complex land-and-sea food web of the Galápagos Islands
ecosystem is supported by food-energy producers (phytoplankton)
and the tiny zooplankton animals that consume them.

Zooplankton

Mini-swimmers—
most no bigger
than the head of a pin—
drift in,
wander in,
kick their feet and feast within
their floating phytoplankton banquet.

Copepods and krill are the most abundant zooplankton
in the world's oceans.

Marine Iguanas

Basking on a sun-soaked ledge,
spike-backed reptiles
raise knobbled heads,
clamber forward on fearsome claws,
leap and launch from lava rocks' edge,
swim off into heaving surge—
marine iguanas submerge.

Flat-oar tails whip side to side,
powering their seabed garden dive—
marine iguanas arrive.

Clinging to boulders with steadfast grip,
scaly heads tilt as razor teeth rip
and gnaw and graze and munch and munch
dinosaur lizards' leafy seaweed lunch.

The marine iguana is an herbivore (plant eater) whose body is heated and cooled by its surroundings. It is the only marine (saltwater) lizard on Earth.

Filter Feeders

Zooplankton multiply,
ocean cools,
sardines tornado in
synchronized schools.

Slim fish swim with
mouths open wide,
swarming silver appetites
satisfied.

Plankton-feeding whale shark
looms into view.
School bus–sized appetite
satisfied too.

Filter feeders of all sizes use special sieves in their
bodies to filter plankton from seawater.

Pacific creolefish pick zooplankton from seawater one at a time.

Nibblers
morsel by morsel
zooplankton nibblers
choose carefully

Cleaner fish such as barberfish and king angelfish pick tasty parasites from the skin or gills of larger fish—even scalloped hammerheads!

Galápagos Penguins

On land they stand umbrella pose,
creating shade to cool their toes,
but underwater, watch them *fly*—
The penguin squadron rockets by!

They hop down from the lava shore,
Galápagos, off Ecuador.
Fish play it safe in schools . . . well, *try* . . .
when penguin squadrons rocket by.

With upward chase, they make a pass
at picking from the twisting mass
of rich sardines or tasty mullets,
open bills, then (*gulp*) down gullets!

Pelicans plummet from the sky,
boobies pelt, then wheel up high,
noddies swoop in, never shy,
cormorants, tuna, sharks, all try
to join the frenzy when they spy
the zooming, fishing, soaring, flipping,
penguin rocket squadron
                    zipping by!

Pacific sardines, mullets, black-striped salema, and other small schooling fish provide food energy for larger-bodied consumers in the Galápagos food web.

Blue-Footed Booby

Dry season's near-shore seas
teem with sardines and creolefish,
favored by a fleet of flying divers
whose island colony will soon sing
with tender offerings—
finest nesting stones and sticks,
lifted tail and wingtips,
whistles, bills raised to the sky,
turquoise fan feet stepping high—
signs of health and hope
to please the eye
of a partner for life.

Blue-footed boobies fish close
to shore, preferring sardines
and Pacific creolefish.

Nazca boobies dive for sardines farther
from shore, between islands.

Nazca Booby

Farther from shore,
grand, white-feathered divers
fold black-tipped wings
to plunge—
    beak-mask-SPLASH!
into seas between islands,
fishing for
(or *wishing* for)
rich, delicious sardines
to nourish one hungry chick
nestling cliffside.

The small, red-footed boobies fish farthest out to sea.
Their diet of flying fish and squid is less nutritious
than sardines.

Each species of booby has its own fishing grounds.

Red-Footed Booby

Miles from outermost islands' edges,
miles from their nests in scrubby trees,
nimble cruisers—
brown or white, petite—
tuck brilliant scarlet feet,
then dive,
to pluck flying fish
and purpleback squid
from night-shadowy, open seas.

Galápagos Sea Lion Pups

Good morning! Hello there! Hiya! Hey!
Our sea lion mamas are fishing for prey
at the all-you-can-eat sardine buffet.
Too young to hunt, we stay safe in our bay.
Another pup fun-day is underway!

Barrel rolls, somersaults, flip-turns, then—
 Say . . .
marine iguana, come on, let's play!
We'll chase, and *you* try to row away
while we nip at your oar of a tail, okay?
No? Not today?
No worries, no matter,
we'll find black-striped salemas to scatter!

When well-fed mamas swim beachward—*hooray!*
We break from our mischief-filled water ballet
to nurse, snug and snoozy, at close of day.

These furred marine mammals sometimes team up to herd large tuna into rocky coves if schooling fish are scarce.

When animals such as sea lions and seabirds poop on shore, nutrients from their seafood diets enrich island soils and help land plants grow.

Galápagos Shark

Muscle-driven teeth
prowl the tropical Pacific.
Finfish scatter.
Marine iguanas, sea lions,
seek lava shores.

Galápagos sharks are carnivores that
hunt a wide variety of ocean dwellers.

Season's Change

Phytoplankton,
zooplankton,
schooling fish,
krill.

Marine food webbers
gobble their fill.

Mini-critters,
big critters,
critters bigger still,
filter-feeding, foraging, flourishing,
until . . .

wet season sets in.

Warm Ocean . . .

Near the turn of each new year,
breeze by breeze,
Pacific trade winds shift,
begin to ease.
A warm surface current drifts
through Galápagos seas
as cool currents slow,
keeping the rich nutrients
needed by sun-powered phytoplankton
    beyond reach,
        deep below.

Species that support the marine food web are less abundant during the Galápagos wet season.

Land species thrive during wet season.

. . . Wet Season

Seas calm,
waters warm,

e v a p o r a t e.

Warmed air rises,
rainclouds form,

p r e c i p i t a t e.

Afternoon upland storms
flow downslope to arid lowlands.
By and by,
black lava islands
parade fresh emeralds and jades,
and soon bloom with yellow-gold.

Even grey matplants,
scraggling across fields of volcanic ash,
wear tiny new leaves
and pearl-blossom crowns,
under sapphire skies.

Large Painted Locust

with a hind-legged *leap*
bold-patterned chewer meets
tender green leaf

This large plant-eating insect makes a welcome mouthful
for many Galápagos land predators.

Prickly Pear Cactus

so much depends
upon

a black carpenter
bee

sipping sweet
nectar

among yellow
flowers

Many prickly pear species found only in the Galápagos
are keystone species providing food, moisture, shade,
and nest sites for most land animals in the arid zone—
the large hot and dry area on each island.

The cactus's yellow flowers attract its most important
pollinator, the carpenter bee.

Giant Tortoises, Ecosystem Managers

After mealtimes, giants rest.
They like a swampy wallow best.
Tromping swampward, footfalls slow,
they trample plants. Those plants won't grow.
These giants till the soil by *feet*,
then sow the seeds they can't digest.

Galápagos tortoises enlarge water holes when they wallow, and their heavy footfalls help plant prickly pear and other seeds they've passed in their dung.

Dome-shelled tortoises graze the grasses and low plants growing in their moist highland habitats.

Galápagos Giant Tortoises

Rain-plumped
prickly pear pads
provide succulent sustenance
for saddle-backed
giants.

To succeed on older, weathered islands, tortoises' shells slowly
evolved from dome shapes into saddle shapes that allowed
them to stretch their necks to reach the tall prickly pear cacti
growing in those hotter, drier landscapes.

Land Iguana Hatchlings

Nestled in volcanic ash,
soft eggs split. A daring dash
from barren berth where no plants grow—
iguana hatchlings hatch and *GO!*

Up crater's rim where hawks may hover,
sprint downslope toward food plants, cover.
Speedy racer snake won't slow, so
bite-sized hatchlings hatch and *GO!*

Threatened, famished, in thin skin
is how these youngsters' lives begin.
Must grown iguanas scurry? No!
But hatchlings hatch and go, GO, *GO!*

The tough, scaly skin of adult land iguanas
discourages natural predators.

Young land iguanas eat insects and small-leaved plants.
Adults rely on fallen prickly pear pads and other vegetation.

Galápagos land iguanas have yellow and brown skin. A rare pink-skinned species is found only on Isabela Island's Wolf Volcano.

Galápagos Finches

Seed picker, fruit shredder, flower sipper.
Insect tweezer, seed cruncher, twig dipper.

Over time,
slight shape changes—
finch beak variations—
can open new food options.
That's adaptation!

Adaptations that help one species survive and
reproduce in the different environment of a new
place—like a nearby island—form a group of new
species known as an adaptive radiation.

SMALL TREE FINCH

COMMON CACTUS FINCH

MEDIUM GROUND FINCH

Fourteen new finches evolved across islands from the accidental arrival of a single species.

Though specimen collections made in the Galápagos and South America by Charles Darwin and his HMS *Beagle* voyage shipmates eventually contributed to Darwin's theory of evolution, these birds, also known as "Darwin's finches," are in the tanager family.

WOODPECKER FINCH

MEDIUM TREE FINCH

VEGETARIAN FINCH

Lava Lizard

Slim. Quick.
Tongue flicks.
GULP!
Goodbye, pesky fly.
Sea lion winks:
thanks!

Hide, dart.
New hunt starts.
POUNCE!
Commence with head-first swallow.
Painted locust body parts
      follow.

Lava lizards primarily eat insects and
the tender nutritious leaves of plants.

Galápagos Centipedes

Wiggle-legged predators
slither out of crevices,
hunt by night.

Wielding stabby venom claws
they fell their lava lizard meals
with pinching "bite."

Galápagos centipedes use a pair of
pointed claws near their heads called
forcipules to stab and inject venom into
lava lizards, nestling birds, and native
rice rats, as well as insects and spiders.

Galápagos Hawk

High on a branch,
top predator perches.
Watches.
Soon launches on air,
silent flap-flap-soar
toward marine iguanas
basking on rocks,
unaware.

Nearby,
mockingbirds cry:
Flee! Flee!
Flee hook-tipped beak!
Flee grip-taloned feet!

Now upright, alert,
iguanas scatter,
retreat.

The Galápagos hawk hunts marine iguanas, seabirds, and every animal in the land food web except adult tortoises and adult land iguanas. It also scavenges meals from dead animals.

Sally Lightfoot Crab

Tender young crabs cling,
dark against black lava,
awaiting brighter days,
when—
as color-splashed adults
on tiptoes, tough—
they'll stuff
seaweed-critters-carrion-bird eggs-guano
by the mouthful,
tidying the intertidal.

Sally lightfoots use their strong claws to pick bothersome
ticks from the skin of marine iguanas.

Lava lizards prey upon young, softer-shelled crabs, but *adult* Sally
lightfoots can eat lava lizards, making a Galápagos food *loop*.

Ghost Crab

On the beach
where sea meets land,
as season meets season,
stalk-eyed scavengers
skitter from tunnel burrows
to sift for scraps,
leaving bead after bead
of cleaned sand
with the message:
Ghost patrol was here.

Swarms of ghost crabs also scavenge
and pick flesh from larger carcasses.

Season Changes Again

Sun-bright blossoms,
juicy cactus,
insect throngs.

Galápagos finches
singing sweet songs.

Herbivores to predators
growing strong,
island food web humming along,

until . . .

dry season returns.

Galápagos: A Delicate Balance

For reasons not well understood,

in some years

a new season

won't arrive

as it should.

At the turn of some years, trade winds don't strengthen as expected. Cold currents can't push cool nourishment upward into warm island waters. Plankton are not plentiful. The marine food web suffers as warm season lasts and lasts in a climate pattern known as El Niño.

In other years, dry season's strong trade winds never quiet. Island waters remain cool. There is no warmed air to rise to cloudburst. Cactus pads wither and land critters hunger and thirst during La Niña climate events.

Worldwide, climate change is contributing to an increase in extreme weather events such as storms, floods, heat waves, and droughts. Climate scientists are concerned that El Niño and La Niña events may occur more often and last longer. Typical seasonal weather patterns may also change. These changes upset the balance between warm and cool, wet and dry, land and sea. The Galápagos ecosystem depends upon this complex balance.

Isolated from the mainland, these volcanic islands had no record of human visitors until about five hundred years ago. At first, humans fished and hunted whales, fur seals, and tortoises until few remained. We brought goats, pigs, dogs, cats, and stowaway rats that became feral (wild). These new feral mammals had no natural predators and reproduced quickly. They devoured small animals, or gobbled prickly pear cacti needed for food, water, and shelter by giant tortoises, land iguanas, finches, and others. Our crops escaped planted boundaries to invade lush highlands where endemic giant daisy trees lost ground.

We humans are learning to conserve Earth's resources, including its valuable biodiversity and unique ecosystems. Currently, 97 percent of Galápagos land and a newly expanded area of surrounding ocean waters — including an important swimway for migratory species — are protected by the Ecuadorian government as the Galápagos National Park and the Galápagos Marine Reserve. Conservationists continue to work on the removal of invasive animals from the islands and have reintroduced giant tortoises raised in captivity to islands where they had become extinct.

Many challenges remain. Visitors wander among the islands' wonders in greater numbers, which provides jobs and increases the need for imported food and other services. Invasive species arrive attached to ships' hulls, on imported fruits and vegetables, and on the soles of travelers' shoes. Plastic trash and particles harm animals throughout the marine food web. Overfishing by foreign fleets at the edges of the marine reserve remains a concern, while the livelihoods of local Galápagos fishers can be impacted by marine reserve expansion.

As we write the next chapters of our human impact on the Galápagos, let them be filled with stories that increase our knowledge of, respect for, and ability to conserve and restore the delicate balance within the Galápagos and our entire ecosystem: Earth.

We are Earth's stewards and protectors.
At every crossroad, our choices matter.
Our fragile ecosystem is in danger.
Let's choose a sustainable future, together.

Galápagos Glossary

biodiversity—the different species of animals and plants that live in one area and their interactions

carcass—the body of a dead animal; plural: carcasses

carrion—the dead or decomposing flesh of an animal

castaway—a person who swims or floats to shore after a shipwreck

current—a stream of water that moves with its own direction and speed within a larger body of water

ecosystem—a community of organisms and their interactions with each other and with the nonliving parts of their environment

El Niño—an extreme weather condition in the Pacific Ocean with reduced cold current upwellings often accompanied by extended rainfall

evolution—gradual changes in the characteristics or traits of a species over time and through generations

food web—interconnected pathways describing the movement of food energy through a community of organisms, from primary producers through top-level consumers (predators) and decomposers

guano—digestive waste produced by seabirds and bats

hotspot—a hot area containing melted magma in the mantle layer below Earth's outer layer

intertidal—pertaining to an area between the low tide mark and the high tide mark of a sea or ocean shoreline; also a noun: the intertidal

La Niña—an extreme weather condition in the Pacific Ocean characterized by extended cold current upwellings and reduced rainfall

mammal—a furred or hairy vertebrate animal that makes internal heat to maintain constant body temperature and produces milk to nourish its infants; nearly all mammals give birth to live young

nutrient—a fundamental substance an organism needs to function and grow

parasite—an organism that depends on an unrelated host organism for food and/or protection, usually harming the host

photosynthesis—the process by which organisms such as phytoplankton and green plants use energy from sunlight to make their own food

phytoplankton—microscopic one-celled organisms that live in oceans and lakes and can use energy from the sun for photosynthesis; some phytoplankton are more closely related to plants, and some to bacteria

pollinator—an animal such as an insect, bird, or bat that carries pollen grains from the male part of a flower (the anther) to the female part (the stigma), helping the plant make fruit or seeds

primary producer—the foundation organism of a food web that is able to use light or chemical energy to make food energy

surge—a powerful swell of a wave against a shore

sustainable—meeting the social, economic, and environmental needs of current and future members of an ecosystem; able to maintain a responsive and responsible balance

trade wind—a steady wind blowing toward the equator

understory—plants and shrubs growing below the upper canopy of vegetation in a forest

zooplankton—tiny animals living in oceans and lakes that float or swim weakly and are carried by currents and tides

THE GALÁPAGOS ISLANDS

WOLF AND DARWIN ISLANDS

PINTA

GENOVESA

MARCHENA

SANTIAGO

BARTOLOMÉ

THE DAPHNES   NORTH SEYMOUR

RÁBIDA   BALTRA

FERNANDINA   THE PLAZAS

PINZÓN

SANTA CRUZ

SANTA FÉ

SAN CRISTÓBAL

ISABELA

FLOREANA

ESPAÑOLA

NORTH AMERICA

SOUTH AMERICA

AFRICA

Poetry Notes

Cool Ocean . . . is written in *free verse*, a poetic form with no pattern of rhyme or rhythm. The letters of the word "upwelling" follow water's movement upward, which is an element of a concrete poem or shape poem.

. . . Dry Season is free verse written in four *stanzas*, or sets of lines. It contains *partial rhyme*—words that share a final vowel sound or a consonant sound, but not both (example: "slopes" and "coast"). The poem also uses *internal rhyme*—rhyme sounds in the middles of lines instead of at their ends. "Cloudburst downpours" in the second stanza is one example.

Phytoplankton is a three-line poem in a Spanish form of poetry called a *soledad*. Spanish is the main language spoken in the Galápagos Islands. A soledad has three lines, with eight *syllables* (parts of words) in each line: Trans/PA/rent/GE/o/MET/ric/FORMS. The first and third lines of a soledad rhyme.

Zooplankton is a short free-verse poem that uses *repetition* of "in" (drift in, wander in, feast within) to emphasize the image of zooplankton surrounded by their food source.

Marine Iguanas is a rhyming poem with no regular pattern in a form I like to call "*free rhyme*."

Filter Feeders is written in three stanzas with four lines in each. The end words in the second and fourth lines of each stanza that rhyme with each other are called *end rhymes*.

Nibblers is written in the ancient Japanese poem form called *haiku*. In Japanese haiku, each of the three nonrhyming lines have a set number of syllables (5-7-5). English-language haiku poets may use three short lines to refer to a moment in nature, keeping the total syllable count to fewer than 17 in all.

Galápagos Penguins is a free-rhyme poem with three stanzas of four lines each and a final stanza that breaks the pattern. The first three stanzas each have two rhyming *couplets*. A couplet contains two lines.

Blue-Footed Booby, Nazca Booby, and **Red-Footed Booby** are all written in free verse with no regular rhythm or rhyme pattern, though each employs the poetic elements of internal, partial, or *perfect rhyme*.

Galápagos Sea Lion Pups is a rhyming poem that follows a rhythm pattern of four STRONG beats in each line.
Good MORning! HelLO there! HIya! HEY!
Our SEA lion MAmas are FIshing for PREY.

Galápagos Shark is written in the ancient Japanese poem form called a *tanka*. This form counts syllables in each of its five nonrhyming lines (5-7-5-7-7). English-language tanka poets may use five short lines and keep the total syllable count to fewer than 31. I like to use a center "turning" line that can make the first three or last three lines each read as a three-line haiku.

Season's Change is written in very short lines. It could also be viewed as four longer rhyming lines with four strong beats in each line:
PHYtoplankton, ZOoplankton, SCHOOLing fish, KRILL
MarINE food WEBbers GOBble their FILL.
The fifth line doesn't rhyme, nor does it follow the four-beat rhythm. Can you figure out why?

Warm Ocean . . . and . . . Wet Season are free verse poems introducing the Galápagos wet season that echo the opening poems introducing the Galápagos dry season.

Large Painted Locust is a haiku, the same form as the poem "Nibblers."

Prickly Pear Cactus is inspired in form and meaning by the well-known sixteen-word poem "The Red Wheelbarrow," written by poet William Carlos Williams and published in 1923.

Giant Tortoises, Ecosystem Managers is written in a free-rhyme style using rhythmic four-beat lines that remind me of the heavy, stomping footsteps of giant tortoises.

Galápagos Giant Tortoises is written in a form that reminds me of a *cinquain*, a poetic form based on Japanese poem forms and created by the American poet Adelaide Crapsey. A cinquain has five lines with the syllable pattern 2, 4, 6, 8, 2. This poem's five lines and syllable count of 2, 4, 8, 4, 2 has a similar feel.

Land Iguana Hatchlings is written in three stanzas with four lines — two rhyming couplets — in each stanza. The last line in each stanza ends in a *refrain*, or repeated line: ". . . hatchlings hatch and *GO!*"

Galápagos Finches is an example of free rhyme.

Lava Lizard is also written in free rhyme.

Galápagos Centipedes is written in two stanzas with three lines in each. The first two lines in each stanza are longer and don't rhyme. The third lines in each stanza are shorter and rhyme with each other.

Galápagos Hawk is a free rhyme poem containing end rhyme, partial rhyme, and many harsh or sharp sounds such as *CH*, *K*, *KS*, and *T*.

Sally Lightfoot Crab is written in nonrhyming free verse.

Ghost Crab is another example of nonrhyming free verse.

Season Changes Again is written in short lines that could also be read as four longer, rhyming lines ending in "throngs," "songs," "strong," and "along." The final line stops the rhyme and rhythm pattern, and mirrors the final pattern-breaking line in the poem "Season's Change" earlier in the book.

Galápagos: A Delicate Balance begins with a poem that introduces readers to a longer, expository section. The final poem is a message about our very human responsibility for planet Earth.

Toward a Sustainable Future for the Galápagos Islands

The Charles Darwin Foundation

darwinfoundation.org/en/

The Charles Darwin Foundation (CDF) is an international non-profit formed in agreement with the Ecuadorian government in 1959. This date marked the one-hundred-year anniversary of the publication of Darwin's theory of evolution, *On the Origin of Species*, inspired by his visit to the Galápagos in 1835. The CDF provides scientific and technical assistance to promote conservation, restoration, and sustainability of natural and social systems through invasive species research, giant tortoise breeding, and other critical initiatives at its Charles Darwin Research Center on Santa Cruz Island and throughout the Galápagos.

The Galápagos Conservancy

galapagos.org

The Galápagos Conservancy is a US-based nonprofit scientific and advocacy organization that partners with the CDF, the Galápagos National Park, local communities, sustainable tourism companies, international universities, and international Galápagos conservation organizations to support equitable and sustainable preservation, protection, and restoration of the Galápagos Islands ecosystem. The Conservancy supports ongoing research on a wide variety of island species, and sponsors the world's largest rewilding project—the reintroduction of giant Galápagos tortoises to islands where the species had previously been extinguished. The Conservancy's Education for Sustainability program provides intensive professional development and practice opportunities for K-12 teachers in the Galápagos.

For Further Reading

Chin, Jason. *Island: A Story of the Galápagos*. New York: Macmillan, 2012. A beautifully illustrated picture book describing the geologic and natural history of the island archipelago, including diagrams, maps, and back matter.

De Roy, Tui. *A Lifetime in Galápagos*. Princeton: Princeton University Press, 2020. Photographic and written natural history observations honed over fifty years in the Galápagos Islands by this renowned photographer, writer, and conservationist.

Fitter, Julian, Daniel Fitter, and David Hosking. *Wildlife of the Galápagos*. Princeton: Princeton University Press, 2016. A photo-illustrated, in-depth wildlife and naturalist guide for visitors and those interested in learning about the Galápagos Islands.

Thermes, Jennifer. *Charles Darwin's Around-the-World Adventure*. New York: Abrams, 2016. In this picture book, detailed illustrations, maps, timeline, and text describe Darwin's momentous sailing voyage on the HMS *Beagle*.

Further Reading on the Web

amnh.org/exhibitions/darwin/educator-resources

The American Museum of Natural History's companion resources to its traveling Darwin exhibition, with extensive information about Darwin and evolution for all grade levels.

discoveringgalapagos.org.uk/

The Galápagos Conservation Trust, a UK-based research and conservation organization, and the Royal Geographical Society have partnered to create "Discovering Galápagos," a bilingual multimedia educational resource that covers diverse topics for students and educators, including evolution, ecology, food webs, plate tectonics, and more.

galapagos.org/about_galapagos

The Galápagos Conservancy offers a wealth of information about the history, geography, and biodiversity of the Galápagos Islands ecosystem.

biointeractive.org/classroom-resources/origin-species-beak-finch

This 16-minute video created for secondary students introduces evolution and speciation in the context of the Galápagos Islands in clear and concise terms. Princeton evolutionary biologists Rosemary and Peter Grant share their study of recent adaptive changes in finch beak size and shape on one island, Daphne Major.

Acknowledgments

My hands-on research for this book was the privilege and adventure of a lifetime. An ocean of gratitude to my number one dive buddy and husband, Rubin Hirsch, for leaping aboard with me.

Many thanks to the skilled scuba instructors, captain, and crew of our dive boat for an incomparable experience, made lovelier in the company of our engaging and enthusiastic dive buddies. Thanks also to the knowledgeable Galápagos National Park guide, captain, crew, and companion explorers who shared our naturalist cruise.

I am immeasurably grateful to Dr. James Gibbs of the Galápagos Conservancy for the honor of his invaluable input right before he headed for Española Island to count tortoises and albatross!

Ongoing appreciation to Peachtree Publishing Company and my dear writing group for joining me on this remarkable journey.

Galápagos: *Islands of Change Species List*

barberfish (*Johnrandallia nigrirostris*) [1]

black carpenter bee (*Xylocopa darwini*)*

black-striped salema (*Xenocys jessiae*)*

blow fly (*Calliphoridae spp.*)* [2]

blue-footed booby (*Sula nebouxii excisa*)*

brown pelican (*Pelecanus occidentalis urinator*)*

flightless cormorant (*Nannopterum harrisi*)*

flying fish (*Cheilopogon atrisignis*)

Galápagos barn owl (*Tyto alba punctatissima*)*

Galápagos centipede (*Scolopendra galapagoensis*)*

Galápagos finches (*Camarhynchus spp., Certhidea spp., Geospiza spp., Platyspiza crassirostris*)*

Galápagos giant tortoise (*Chelonoidis spp.*)*

Galápagos hawk (*Buteo galapagoensis*)*

Galápagos mockingbird (*Mimus spp.*)*

Galápagos penguin (*Spheniscus mendiculus*)*

Galápagos racer snake (*Pseudalsophis spp.*)*

Galápagos sea lion (*Zalophus wollebaeki*)*

Galápagos shark (*Carcharhinus galapagensis*)

ghost crab (*Ocypode gaudichaudii*)

giant daisy tree (*Scalesia spp.*)*

grey matplant (*Tiquilia spp.*)*

Galápagos pink land iguana (*Conolophus marthae*)*

Galápagos land iguana (*Conolophus subcristatus*)*, also Santa Fé land iguana (*Conolophus pallidus*)*

king angelfish (*Holacanthus passer*)

large painted locust (*Schistocerca melanocera*)*

lava lizard (*Microlophus spp.*)*

marine iguana (*Amblyrhynchus cristatus*)*

mullet (*Mugil spp.*)

Nazca booby (*Sula granti*)

noddy (brown noddy) (*Anous stolidus galapagensis*)*

Pacific creolefish (*Paranthias colonus*)

Pacific sardine (*Sardinops sagax*)

prickly pear cactus (*Opuntia spp.*)*

purpleback squid (*Sthenoteuthis oualaniensis*)

red-footed booby (*Sula sula websteri*)

rice rat (*Aegialomys galapagoensis, Nesoryzomys spp.*)*

Sally lightfoot crab (*Grapsus grapsus*)

scalloped hammerhead shark (*Sphyrna lewini*)

whale shark (*Rhincodon typus*)

yellowfin tuna (*Thunnus albacares*)

* includes an endemic species or subspecies

[1] scientific names of organisms are written in the form (*Genus species*) or (*Genus species subspecies*)

[2] the notation "spp." written after a genus name refers to two or more different species with that genus group. Here, (*Calliphoridae spp.*) refers to more than one species of blow fly in the genus *Calliphoridae*.